A note on Baking Muffins

Unless otherwise stated, the method for
making muffin batter is to mix the dry and
moist ingredients separately; and then to
combine both mixtures. Mix only until the dry
ingredients are moistened (the batter at this
point should be slightly lumpy).

A. Marks

Canadian Cataloguing in Publication Data

Marks, Adele, 1929-
  101 marvelous muffins

Includes index.

ISBN 0-9690579-1-1

1. Muffins.   I. Title.

TX769.M37   641.8'15   C82-095096-3

Table of Contents

Apple Caraway Muffins

Ingredients: (makes 12 large)

1 1/3 cups all purpose flour	301 g.
2 tbsp. baking powder	28 g.
3/4 tsp. salt	4 g.
1/2 tsp. baking soda	3 g.
2/3 cup rye flour	151 g.
2 tsp. caraway seed	9 g.
1/4 tsp. pepper	2 g.
1/4 cup softened butter	56 ml.
1/4 cup sugar	56 g.
2 eggs	same
3/4 cup sour cream	169 ml.
1/3 cup apple juice	75 ml.
1/2 tsp. almond flavor	3 ml.
1 1/2 cups peeled, cored, finely diced tart apple	339 g.

1. Preheat oven to 400°F (204°c)
2. In a large bowl sift together first 4 ingredients
3. Add next 3 ingredients, stir and set aside
4. In a separate bowl, cream butter until fluffy
5. Beat sugar into butter 1 tbsp. at a time until fluffy
6. Beat in eggs one at a time
7. Add sour cream, juice, and almond flavor
8. Add the moist mixture to the dry ingredients
9. Stir just until combined
10. Fold in apple
11. Spoon batter into well greased muffin tins (2/3 full)
12. Bake for 20 to 25 minutes

Apple Cheese Muffins

Ingredients: (makes 12)

2 cups sifted all purpose flour . . . . 452g.

1½ tsp. baking powder. . . . . 8 g.

½ tsp. baking soda. . . . . 3g.

1 tsp. salt. .5g.

½ cup butter or margarine softened . . . . 113ml.

⅔ cup sugar. . . . . 151g.

2 eggs. . . . . same

1 cup peeled, cored, finely shredded apple. . . . .226g.

½ cup shredded cheddar cheese (medium). . . . . . 113 g.

1. Preheat oven to 350°F (177°C)
2. Sift first 4 ingredients together in a large bowl
3. In a separate bowl combine next 4 ingredients
4. Add moist mixture to dry ingredients all at once
5. Stir just until combined, do not overmix
6. Fold in cheese
7. Spoon butter into greased muffin tins
8. Bake 20 to 25 minutes or until springy to touch

Apple Lemon Muffins

Ingredients: (makes 12 large)

1 cup all purpose flour, sifted	226 g.
1½ tsp. baking powder	8 g.
½ tsp. baking soda	3 g.
½ tsp. salt	3 g.
½ tsp. cinnamon	3 g.
½ tsp. grated nutmeg	3 g.
¼ cup pecans, chopped fine	56 g.
1 peeled, cored, chopped, tart apple	same
2 tbsp. grated lemon peel	28 g.
2/3 cup sugar	151 g.
2 eggs	same
¼ cup vegetable oil	56 ml.
2 tsp. lemon juice	9 ml.
½ tsp. vanilla	3 ml.

1. Preheat oven to 350°F (177°c)
2. Combine first 7 ingredients in a large bowl, mix and set aside
3. Combine 7 remaining ingredients in a separate bowl, and mix
4. Add liquid mixture to dry, all at once
5. Stir just until dry ingredients are moistened
6. Spoon batter into greased muffin tins
7. Bake about 20 to 25 minutes or until firm to the touch

Apple 'n' Almond Muffins

Ingredients: (makes 12 medium)

2 eggs.	same
½ cup vegetable oil.	113ml.
¾ cup brown sugar, packed	169g.
½ tbsp. vanilla.	7ml.
½ tbsp. almond flavor	7ml.
1 cup grated, peeled apple; firmly packed	226g.
¾ cup all purpose flour.	169g.
¾ cup whole wheat flour.	169g.
½ tsp. baking soda	3g.
½ tsp. baking powder.	3g.
½ tsp. salt.	3g.
¾ tsp. cinnamon	4g.
½ cup chopped toasted almonds.	113g.

1. Preheat oven to 350°F (177°C)
2. In a large bowl combine first 6 ingredients
3. In a separate large bowl, sift together next 6 ingredients
4. Add moist mixture to dry ingredients all at once
5. Stir just until dry ingredients are moistened
6. Fold in almonds
7. Spoon batter into greased muffin cups
8. Bake for 25 minutes

Apple-Orange Muffins

Ingredients: (makes 12)

3/4 cup orange juice	169 ml.
1/3 cup vegetable oil	75 ml.
1/2 cup sugar	113 g.
1 egg, beaten	same
1 tbsp. grated orange rind	14 g.
1 tsp. vanilla	5 ml.
2 cups sifted all purpose flour	452 g.
1 tsp. baking powder	5 g.
1/2 tsp. baking soda	3 g.
1/2 tsp. salt	3 g.
1/2 cup raisins	113 g.
1/4 cup chopped nuts	56 g.
1 cup finely chopped tart apple	226 g.

1. Preheat oven to 350°F (177°C)
2. Combine first 6 ingredients together in a large bowl
3. In a separate bowl, sift next 4 dry ingredients together
4. Add dry ingredients to wet mixture
5. Stir just enough to moisten dry ingredients
6. Fold in remaining ingredients
7. Spoon batter into greased muffin tins
8. Bake for 25 minutes

Apple Pie Muffins

Ingredients: (makes 15)

½ cup brown sugar	113 g.
6 tbsp. flour	84 g.
¼ cup butter	56 ml.
1 tsp. cinnamon	5 g.
1½ cups firmly packed brown sugar	339 g.
⅔ cup vegetable oil	151 ml.
1 egg	same
1 cup buttermilk	226 ml.
1 tsp. baking soda	5 g.
1 tsp. salt	5 g.
1 tsp. vanilla	5 ml.
2½ cups sifted all purpose flour	565 g.
2 cups peeled, diced apple	452 g.
½ cup chopped toasted pecans	113 g.

1. Preheat oven to 325°F (163°C)
2. Grease and flour muffin tins
3. Combine first 4 ingredients in a small bowl, mix until crumbly. Reserve this topping
4. Combine next 3 ingredients in a separate bowl, (mix A).
5. Combine buttermilk, soda, salt, and vanilla in another bowl, (mix B). Blend flour into mix A, alternately with mix B. Stir until just combined. Fold in apple and pecans.
6. Place batter in tins; sprinkle with topping mix
7. Bake for 25 minutes or until tops spring back

Apple Spice Muffins

Ingredients: (makes 12 two inch)

2/3 cup apple juice	151 ml.
1 egg, slightly beaten	same
1/4 cup oil	56 ml
1 tsp. vanilla	5 ml
1 tbsp. grated lemon rind	14 g.
2 cups flour	452 g.
1/4 cup + 2 tbsp. sugar	84 g.
1 tbsp. baking powder	14 g.
3/4 tsp. salt	4 g.
3/4 tsp. pumpkin pie spice	4 g.
1 cup chopped peeled apple	226 g.
1/2 cup golden raisins	113 g.

1. In a small bowl combine first 5 ingredients
2. In a medium bowl combine next 5 ingredients
3. Add juice mix all at once to dry ingredients
4. Stir just until moistened
5. Fold in apples and raisins
6. Spoon batter into greased muffin tins
7. Bake at 425°F (218°C) 20 to 25 minutes
8. Cool on a rack

Applesauce Cinnamon Muffins

Ingredients: (makes 12)

½ cup softened butter or margarine . . . . 113 ml.
½ cup sugar. . . . . .113 g.
2 eggs . . . . .same
¾ cup applesauce. . . . . 339 ml.
1¾ cups all purpose flour. . . . . .395 g.
3 tsp. baking powder. . . . . .14 g.
½ tsp. cinnamon . . . . .3 g.
½ tsp. salt . . . . .3 g.
¼ cup melted butter or margarine . . . . .56 ml.
½ cup sugar . . . . 113 g.
1 tsp. cinnamon . . . . .5 g.

1. Preheat oven to 425°F (218°C)
2. In a large bowl cream butter and sugar together
   until fluffy
3. Beat in eggs one at a time until fluffy
4. Beat in applesauce
5. In another bowl combine flour, baking powder,
   cinnamon and salt
6. Add to butter mixture and stir just to moisten
7. Spoon batter into well greased muffin tins
8. Bake 15 minutes or until golden
9. While muffins are warm dip tops into melted
   butter and then into a mixture of sugar
   and cinnamon

Applesauce Oatmeal Muffins

Ingredients: (makes 12)

½ cup butter or margarine	113 ml.
¾ cup brown sugar	169 g.
1 egg	same
1 cup all purpose flour	226 g.
½ tsp. cinnamon	3 g.
1 tsp. baking powder	5 g.
¼ tsp. baking soda	2 g.
¼ tsp. salt	2 g.
¾ cup applesauce	169 ml.
¼ cup golden raisins	56 g.
¼ cup currants	56 g.
1 cup quick cooking rolled oats	226 g.
½ cup chopped pecans	113 g.

omit (bracketing the golden raisins and currants)

1. Preheat oven to 350°F (177°c)
2. In a large bowl cream together first 2 ingredients
3. Add egg, beat well
4. In a separate bowl, sift next 5 ingredients together
5. Add to the creamed mixture alternately with applesauce, mix well
6. Add remaining ingredients, mix well
7. Spoon batter into well buttered muffin cups
8. Bake 25 to 30 minutes or until done
9. Cool on a rack

Apricot Orange Muffins

Ingredients: (makes 12 large)

½ rind of a large orange (white peeled away) . . same
½ cup dried apricots, packed. . . . . .113 g.
½ cup raisins. . . . . .113 g.
½ cup walnuts . . . . .113 g.
1 cup orange juice . . . . .226 ml.
2 eggs, lightly beaten . . . . .same
2 tbsp. melted butter. . . . . 28 ml.
1 tsp. vanilla . . . . .5 ml.
2 cups sifted all purpose flour . . . . 452 g.
2 tsp. baking powder. . . . . .9 g.
1 tsp. baking soda . . . . .5 g.
½ tsp. salt. .3 g.
3/4 cup sugar. . . . . .169 g.

1. Preheat oven to 350°F (177°c)
2. Combine first 4 ingredients in a food chopper,
   chop fine and place in a large mixing bowl
3. Add next 4 liquid ingredients
4. Sift remaining dry ingredients together into the
   moist mixture
5. Stir just to blend
6. Spoon batter into well greased muffin tins
7. Bake 20 to 25 minutes

Almond Banana Muffins

Ingredients: (makes 12)

1 egg	same
1/4 cup sugar	56 g.
1/4 cup soft butter	56 ml.
1 tsp. lemon juice	5 ml.
1 cup very ripe mashed banana	226 ml.
1/2 tsp. almond flavor	3 ml.
1/4 cup milk	56 ml.
1/2 cup chopped toasted almonds	113 g.
1 1/2 cups sifted all purpose flour	339 g.
1 1/2 tsp. baking powder	8 g.
1/2 tsp. baking soda	3 g.
1/4 tsp. salt	2 g.

1. Preheat oven to 375°F (190°C)
2. Grease 12 large muffin cups
3. Beat egg, sugar, and butter together well
4. Add lemon juice to mashed bananas, then add to first mixture
5. Add almond flavor, milk, and chopped almonds
6. Sift flour, baking powder, soda, and salt together into the mixture and stir just enough to blend
7. Spoon batter into muffin cups
8. Bake about 20 minutes or until tops spring back

Banana Bran Muffins

Ingredients: (makes 20)

½ cup softened butter	113 ml.
1 cup sugar	226 g.
3 eggs	same
1 cup bran cereal	226 g.
1 cup mashed banana	226 ml.
⅓ cup yogurt	75 ml.
1¾ cups sifted flour	395 g.
1½ tsp. baking powder	8 g.
½ tsp. baking soda	3 g.
½ tsp. salt	3 g.
½ tsp. cinnamon	3 g.

1. Preheat oven to 350°F (177°C)
2. Cream butter and sugar together well
3. Add eggs one at a time, beat well after each addition
4. In a separate bowl, combine bran, banana, and yogurt
5. Add to the egg mixture
6. Fold in flour, baking powder, baking soda, salt, and cinnamon
7. Pour batter into 2½-inch muffin cups
8. Bake for 25 minutes or until an inserted toothpick comes out clean
9. Transfer to a rack to cool

Banana Cornmeal Muffins

Ingredients: (makes 12)

⅓ cup sugar . . . . 75 g
4 tsp. baking powder . . . . 18 g
½ tsp. salt . . . . 3 g
1 cup cornmeal . . . . 226 g
¾ cup flour plus 2 tbsp. flour . . . . 197 g
¼ cup crumbled banana chips . . . . 56 g
1 egg beaten . . . . same
1 cup milk . . . . 226 ml.
¼ cup oil (vegetable) . . . . 56 ml.

1. Preheat oven to 400°F (204°C)
2. Sift dry ingredients together, include banana chips
3. In another bowl combine egg, milk, and oil
4. Make a well in the dry ingredients
5. Pour in liquid mixture
6. Stir quickly, only until combined, do not overmix
7. Fill greased muffin tins ¾ full
8. Bake 20 to 25 minutes until golden brown

Banana Crunch Muffins

Ingredients: (makes 12 medium)

1. 3/4 cup all purpose flour . . . . 169g.
2. 1/4 cup whole wheat flour. . . . . 56g.
3. 1/2 cup brown sugar. . . . . 113g.
4. 2 1/2 tsp. baking powder. . . . . 21g.
5. 1/2 tsp. salt . . . . .3g.
6. 1/4 tsp. baking soda . . . . .2g.
7. 3/4 cup quick cooking oatmeal . . . . 169g.
8. 1 egg beaten. . . . . .same
9. 3 tbsp. vegetable oil. . . . . 42ml.
10. 3/4 cup sour cream. . . . . 169ml.
11. 1/2 cup mashed banana . . . . 113ml.
12. 1/2 cup chopped dates . . . . 113g.

1. Preheat oven to 400°F (204°C)
2. Combine first 6 ingredients, stir well to blend
3. Stir in oatmeal
4. In a separate bowl combine remaining ingredients
5. Add moist mixture all at once to dry ingredients
6. Stir only until dry ingredients are moistened
7. Fill well greased muffin tins 2/3 full
8. Bake for 18 to 20 minutes until firm

Banana Nut Muffins

Ingredients: (makes 18 medium) 12

1²/₃ 2½ cups all purpose flour	565g.	1.
½ ¾ cup sugar.	169g.	2.
1 1½ tbsp. baking powder.	21 g.	3.
½ ¾ tsp. salt	4 g.	4.
4 6 tbsp. butter, softened	84ml.	
²/₃ 1 cup chopped walnuts	226g.	
2 3 ripe medium bananas, cut in pieces.	same	
1 2 eggs.	same	
¼ ⅓ cup milk	75ml.	
⅓ ½ tsp vanilla extract	3 ml.	

1. Preheat oven to 400°F (204°c)
2. In a large bowl combine first 4 ingredients
3. Cut in butter until mixture resembles coarse crumbs
4. Stir in walnuts, set aside
5. In a blender at high speed combine remaining ingredients; only until bananas are chopped
6. Stir liquid mixture into first (dry) mixture
7. Mix only until moistened, do not overmix
8. Spoon batter into greased muffin cups
9. Bake 25 to 30 minutes until golden

(1) Banana Orange Muffins

Ingredients: (makes 12 medium)

½ cup sugar. . . . . .113 g.
¼ cup vegetable oil . . . . 56ml.
1 cup ripe mashed banana. . . . . 226ml.
¼ cup orange marmelade . . . . 56ml.
1 egg beaten .same
½ cup all purpose flour (sifted) . . . . 113g.
¼ cup whole wheat flour (sifted). . . . . .56g.
¼ cup wheat bran. . . . . .56g.
½ tsp. baking soda . . . . 3g.
¼ tsp. salt . . . . .2g.
¼ cup chopped pecans . . . . .56g.
¼ cup flaked coconut . . . . .56g.
½ cup chopped floured dates . . . . .113g.

1. Preheat oven to 375°F (190°c)
2. Combine first 5 ingredients in a bowl, mix, set aside
3. In a separate large bowl combine remaining ingredients
4. Add liquid mixture to dry ingredients all at once
5. Stir just until dry ingredients are moistened
6. Spoon batter into greased muffin pans
7. Bake 30 to 40 minutes or until springy to touch

Banana Orange Muffins (II)

Ingredients: (makes 18)

1½ cups sifted all purpose flour	339 g.
½ cup sugar	113 g.
3 tsp. baking powder	14 g.
¼ tsp. salt	2 g.
1 cup wheat germ	226 g.
1 cup mashed banana (2 medium)	226 ml.
½ cup orange juice	113 ml.
¼ cup vegetable oil	56 ml.
2 eggs	same
1 tsp. grated orange peel	5 g.
½ cup chopped pecans	113 g.

1. Sift together first 4 ingredients
2. Stir wheat germ into sifted ingredients
3. Make a well in the dry ingredients
4. In a separate bowl, combine remaining ingredients
5. Pour liquid mixture all at once into dry mixture
6. Stir just until moistened, do not overmix
7. Fill well greased muffin cups ¾ full
8. Bake at 400°F (204°C) 20 to 25 minutes until golden

Banana Pecan Muffins

Ingredients: (makes 12)

1½ cups ripe mashed banana (3 large)	339 ml.
¾ cup packed brown sugar.	169 g.
1 egg	same
½ tsp. banana flavor	3 ml.
1½ cups sifted all purpose flour.	339 g.
1 tsp. baking soda.	5 g.
1 tsp. baking powder.	5 g.
½ tsp. salt.	3 g.
2 tbsp. wheat germ.	28 g.
⅓ cup melted butter, cooled	75 ml.
½ cup chopped **pecans**	113 g.

1. Preheat oven to 350°F (177°c)
2. In a large bowl combine first 4 ingredients
3. Beat until smooth
4. In a separate bowl sift together next 4 ingredients
5. Add dry ingredients to banana mixture, stir slightly
6. Stir in wheat germ and melted butter
7. Mix only until ingredients are blended
8. Spoon batter into well greased muffin tins
9. Sprinkle chopped pecans on top of batter
10. Bake for 15 to 20 minutes, or until golden

Banana-Split Muffins

Ingredients: (makes 12)

2 cups biscuit mix	452g.
1/4 cup sugar	.56 g.
2 egg yolks, beaten (reserve whites)	same
2/3 cup milk	.151 ml.
2 tbsp. vegetable oil	.28 ml.
1/2 small banana (cut in 12 pieces)	same
12 maraschino cherries (cut in half)	same
12 walnut halves	same
1/3 cup sugar	75 g.
2/3 cup shredded sweet coconut	151 g.

1. Combine biscuit mix and 1/4 cup sugar
2. In a separate bowl combine egg yolk, milk, and oil
3. Add the liquid mix all at once to the dry ingredients
4. Stir just to moisten
5. Put 1 1/2 tbsp. batter into each greased muffin tin
6. Place a piece of banana, a cherry half, and a walnut half into each muffin tin
7. Place another 1 tbsp. batter in each tin
8. In a separate bowl beat 2 egg whites into soft peaks
9. Gradually add 1/3 cup sugar to the whites and continue to beat into stiff peaks
10. Fold coconut into stiffened whites
11. Place 1 1/2 tbsp. of coconut meringue on top of the batter already in each tin
12. Top with a cherry half
13. Bake at 400°F (204°c) for 15 to 20 minutes

Raisin Banana Muffins

Ingredients: (makes 12)

½ cup sugar	113 g.
6 tbsp. melted shortening or oil	84 ml.
1 cup ripe mashed banana	226ml.
1 egg, beaten	same
1¼ tsp. vanilla	2 ml.
1½ cups whole wheat flour	339g.
1 tsp. baking powder	5 g.
1 tsp. baking soda	5 g.
1 tsp. salt	5 g.
½ cup raisins	113g.
¼ cup chopped walnuts	56g.

1. Combine first 3 ingredients, mix well
2. Beat in egg and vanilla
3. In a separate bowl, sift together flour, baking powder, soda, and salt
4. Stir raisins and walnuts into the dry mixture
5. Lightly stir dry mixture into banana mixture
6. Spoon batter into well greased muffin pans
7. Bake in a preheated oven at 350°F (176°C) for 20 minutes or until tops spring back

Black Bottom Muffins

Ingredients: (makes 18 medium)

1½ cups sifted all purpose flour	339 g.
¼ cup unsweetened cocoa	56 g.
1 tsp. baking soda.	5 g.
1 tsp. cinnamon.	5 g.
½ tsp. salt	3 g.
1 cup sugar.	226 g.
1 egg	same
1 cup water.	226 ml.
½ cup vegetable oil	113 ml.
1 tbsp. vinegar.	14 ml.
2 tsp. vanilla	9 ml.
1 8oz. pkg. cream cheese, softened.	226 g.
1 egg	same
⅓ cup sugar.	75 g.
¼ tsp. salt.	2 g.
⅓ cup slivered blanched almonds, chopped	75 g.

1. Preheat oven to 350°F (177°C)
2. Sift first 5 ingredients together in a large bowl
3. Add sugar, mix slightly
4. In another bowl combine next 5 moist ingredients
5. Add liquid mix to dry, mix until smooth. Place paper liners into greased tins, fill ¾ full with batter
8. In another bowl cream next 4 ingredients together until almost smooth, fold in almonds
9. Place about 2 tsp. of the cheese mixture into each cup, press in slightly
10. Bake 20 to 25 minutes, cool on rack 2 minutes, then remove

Black Cherry Muffins

Ingredients: (makes 12 large)

1½ cups all purpose flour . . . . 339g.
½ cup sugar .113 g.
2½ tsp. baking powder . . . . .11g.
½ tsp. salt . . . . .3g.
1 egg, beaten . . . . same
½ cup milk .113ml.
¼ cup orange juice . . . . 56ml.
3 tbsp. melted butter . . . . 42ml.
½ tsp. almond extract . . . . .3ml.
¾ cup pitted black sweet cherries (if canned, drain well) 169g.
1 tbsp. grated lemon rind . . . . 14g.

1. Preheat oven to 400°F (204°C)
2. Sift first 4 ingredients together in a large bowl
3. Combine next 5 liquid ingredients in a separate bowl
4. Add liquids all at once to dry ingredients
5. Stir just enough to blend; batter should be lumpy
6. Fold in cherries and lemon rind
7. Fill greased muffin tins ⅔ full
8. Bake 15 to 18 minutes or until firm to the touch

Blueberry Buckle Muffins

Ingredients: (makes 12)

¼ cup butter, softened	56ml.
½ cup sugar	113g.
1 egg	same
½ tsp vanilla	3ml.
⅓ cup milk	75ml.
1 cup flour	226g.
1 tsp. baking powder	5g.
¼ tsp. salt	2g.
1½ cups blueberries	339g.
½ tsp. cinnamon	3g.
¼ tsp. nutmeg	2g.
½ cup flour	113g.
¼ cup butter, softened	56ml.
½ cup sugar	113g.
1 tbsp. grated lemon rind	14g.

1. For this recipe use extra deep muffin tins well greased
2. Preheat oven to 350°F (177°c)
3. In a medium bowl combine first 5 ingredients, mix well
4. In a separate bowl combine next 3 dry ingredients
5. Add dry mixture to the moist ingredients, stir only slightly
6. Spoon the batter evenly between 12 tins
7. Divide the blueberries into the 12 tins on top of the batter
8. In another bowl combine the remaining ingredients, mix well
9. Spoon the topping evenly between the 12 tins
10. Bake for 30 minutes, then let cool in tins for 5 minutes
11. Remove carefully from the tins

Blueberry Corn Muffins

Ingredients: (makes 12 three inch)

1 cup cornmeal	226 g.
1 cup flour	226 g.
1/3 cup sugar	75 g.
2 1/2 tsp. baking powder	13 g.
1/4 tsp. salt	2 g.
1 cup milk	226 ml.
3/4 cup blueberries	169 ml.
6 tbsp. melted butter	84 ml.
1 egg lightly beaten	same
2 tsp. grated lemon rind	9 g.

1. Preheat oven to 400°F (204°C)
2. Combine first 5 ingredients in a medium bowl
3. In a separate bowl, combine remaining ingredients
4. Add liquid mix to dry ingredients all at once
5. Stir just until combined
6. Spoon batter into greased muffin cups
7. Bake for 25 to 30 minutes or until golden

Blueberry Oat Muffins

Ingredients: (makes 12 large)

1²/3 cups blueberries.	377 g.
2 tbsp. flour.	28 g.
3/4 cup oatmeal.	169 g.
1 1/2 cups sifted all purpose flour	339 g.
1 cup sugar.	113 g.
1 tbsp. baking powder	14 g.
1 tsp. salt	5 g.
1/2 cup cold butter or margarine, cut into bits. . . .	113 g.
1 1/2 tbsp. grated lemon rind	21 g.
2/3 cup milk	151 ml.
1 egg, beaten	Same
1 1/2 tbsp. sugar	21 g.
2 tsp. cinnamon	9 g.

1. Toss first 2 ingredients together in a small bowl, set aside
2. In a separate large bowl, combine next 5 ingredients, mix well
3. Add butter and lemon rind
4. Blend the mixture until it resembles meal
5. Add the floured blueberries and mix
6. In a separate bowl, combine milk and egg
7. Add to the dry mixture, stir until just combined
8. Spoon batter into buttered muffin cups, fill to 2/3
9. Combine sugar and cinnamon in a small bowl
10. Sprinkle over muffins
11. Bake for 20 to 25 minutes or until puffed and golden

Blueberry Oatmeal Muffins

Ingredients: (makes 12)

1 cup plus 2 tbsp. rolled oats	254 g.
1 cup buttermilk	226 ml.
1 tbsp. vanilla	14 ml.
1 cup whole wheat flour	226 g.
1 tbsp. baking powder	14 g.
1 tsp. salt	5 g.
1 tsp. cinnamon	5 g.
1/2 tsp. baking soda	3 g.
1/2 tsp. nutmeg	3 g.
1/4 cup walnuts, chopped	56 g.
1 egg	same
3/4 cup packed brown sugar	169 g.
1/4 cup unsalted butter, melted	56 ml.
1 1/2 cups blueberries, fresh or frozen	339 g.

1. Preheat oven to 400°F (204°c)
2. In a medium bowl combine first 3 ingredients, let stand
3. In a separate bowl, combine next 6 ingredients
4. Add nuts to dry mix
5. Add egg, brown sugar, and melted butter to first mixture
6. Add entire moist mixture to dry ingredients
7. Stir just until moistened
8. Fold in berries, Spoon batter into greased muffin tins
9. Bake 15 to 20 minutes or until firm

Sugar-Top Blueberry Muffins

Ingredients: (make 12 large)

1/2 cup shortening	113ml.
1 cup sugar	226g.
2 egg yolks	same
1 tsp. vanilla	5ml.
2 stiffly beaten egg whites	same
1 1/2 cups sifted all purpose flour	339g.
1 tsp. baking powder	5g.
1/2 tsp. salt	3g.
1/2 tsp. cinnamon	3g.
1/3 cup milk	75ml.
1 1/2 cups fresh or frozen blueberries, floured	339g.
1 tbsp. sugar	14g.

1. Preheat oven to 350°F (177°c)
2. In a large bowl, cream first 4 ingredients together
3. Fold in stiff whites
4. In another bowl, combine next 4 dry ingredients
5. Add the dry mixture alternately with the milk to the wet ingredients, mixing slightly
6. Fold in the floured blueberries
7. Spoon batter into greased muffin tins
8. Sprinkle sugar evenly over muffins
9. Bake for 20 to 25 minutes

Yogurt Blueberry Muffins

Ingredients: (makes 18 medium)

1 cup all purpose flour	226g.
2 tsp. baking powder	9 g.
1 tsp. baking soda	5 g.
1/4 tsp. salt	2 g.
3/4 cup brown sugar	169g.
1 cup bran	226g.
1 cup yogurt	226ml.
1 egg, beaten	same
1/2 cup oil	113ml.
1 tsp. vanilla	5 ml.
3/4 cup blueberries (fresh or frozen)	169g.

1. Preheat oven to 350°F (177°C)
2. Sift together first 4 ingredients
3. Stir in sugar and bran
4. In a separate bowl combine next 4 ingredients
5. Add liquid mix to dry ingredients all at once
6. Stir only until combined, do not overmix
7. Fold in blueberries
8. Pour batter into greased muffin tins
9. Bake for 35 minutes until firm

Brownie Muffins

Ingredients: *(makes 12 large)*

1. 1½ cups all purpose flour	. . . .	339 g.
2. 1 cup brown sugar	. . . .	226 g.
3. ⅔ cup cocoa	. . . .	151 g.
4. 3 tsp. baking powder	. . . .	14 g.
5. 1 tsp. salt	. . . .	5 g.
6. 1 cup granola cereal	. . . .	226 g.
7 2 eggs	. . . .	same
8 1 cup milk	. . . .	226 ml.
9 ⅓ cup vegetable oil	. . . .	75 ml.
10 1 tsp. vanilla	. . . .	5 ml.

1. Combine first 6 ingredients in a large bowl
2. In another bowl, beat eggs, milk, oil, and vanilla
3. Pour liquid mixture all at once into dry ingredients
4. Stir only until mixed (should be lumpy)
5. Bake in a preheated oven at 375°F (191°c) for 18 to 20 minutes or until firm to touch

Buttermilk Bran Specials

Ingredients: (makes 12)

½ tsp. baking soda	3 g.
½ cup sour cream	113 ml.
1 cup brown sugar	226 g.
½ cup margarine	113 ml.
1 egg	same
1 tsp. vanilla	5 ml.
1¼ cups all purpose flour	282 g.
1 cup all bran cereal	226 g.
2 tsp. baking powder	9 g.
⅓ cup buttermilk	75 ml
½ cup seedless raisins	113 g.

1. Preheat oven to 350°F (177°c)
2. Combine baking soda and sour cream, set aside
3. In a separate bowl beat together next 4 ingredients
4. In another bowl combine next 3 ingredients (dry)
5. Fold dry ingredients alternately with buttermilk into the moist mixture
6. Fold in raisins
7. Fold in soda and sour cream
8. Spoon batter into well greased muffin tins
9. Bake for 25 minutes or until firm

COCONUT

Carrot-Coconut-Cherry Muffins

Ingredients: (makes 12)

1¼ cups all purpose flour.	282 g.
½ cup sugar.	113 g.
½ tsp. baking powder	3 g.
½ tsp. baking soda	3 g.
¼ tsp. salt	2 g.
½ tsp. ground mace	3 g.
2 eggs, beaten	same
¼ cup vegetable oil	56 ml.
¼ cup milk	56 ml.
1¼ cups finely shredded carrots.	282 g.
¾ cup shredded sweetened coconut	169 g.
½ cup maraschino cherries, drained and chopped . .	113 g.

1. Preheat oven to 350°F (177°c)
2. In a large bowl sift together first 6 ingredients
3. In a separate bowl combine next 3 moist ingredients
4. Add moist mixture to dry ingredients all at once
5. Stir just until dry ingredients are moistened
6. Fold in carrots, coconut, and cherries, mix slightly
7. Spoon batter into greased muffin tins
8. Bake for 25 minutes or until tops are springy

Carob Brownie Muffins

Ingredients: (makes 12)

1 3/4 cups all purpose flour	395 g.
2/3 cup sugar	151 g.
1/4 cup carob	56 g.
2 1/2 tsp. baking powder	12 g.
3/4 tsp salt	4 g.
1 tsp. cinnamon	5 g.
1 egg, beaten	same
3/4 cup milk	169 ml.
1/2 cup vegetable oil	113 ml.
1/2 cup chopped nuts	113 g.

1. Preheat oven to 400°F (204°c)
2. Combine first 6 ingredients in a large bowl
3. In a separate bowl combine next 3 moist ingredients
4. Add moist mixture to dry ingredients all at once
5. Stir just until combined
6. Fold in nuts
7. Spoon batter into greased muffin tins
8. Bake for 18 to 20 minutes

Carrot Oatmeal Muffins

Ingredients: (makes 12)

1 cup buttermilk	226ml.
1 cup quick cooking oats	226 g.
1 egg, beaten	same
2/3 cup packed brown sugar	151g.
1/3 cup melted butter	75ml.
3/4 cup finely shredded carrots	169g.
1 tsp. vanilla	5ml.
1 tbsp. grated orange rind	14g.
1 cup whole wheat flour	226g.
1 tbsp. baking powder	14 g.
1/2 tsp. baking soda	3g.
1 tsp. salt	5g.
1/2 cup raisins	113g.

1. Preheat oven to 400°F (204°C)
2. In a small bowl, pour buttermilk over oats
3. Add next 6 ingredients, mix well
4. In a separate bowl combine next 4 ingredients
5. Add dry ingredients to first (moist) mixture
6. Stir just until combined
7. Fold in raisins
8. Spoon batter into greased muffin cups
9. Bake about 20 minutes or until golden

Carrot-tea Muffins

Ingredients: (makes 12)

½ cup white sugar	113 g.
½ cup brown sugar	113 g.
¾ cup vegetable oil	169 ml.
3 eggs	same
1 tbsp. lemon juice	14 ml.
1 tsp. vanilla	5 ml.
2 tsp. grated lemon rind	9 g.
2 cups all purpose flour	452 g.
3½ tsp. baking powder	17 g.
1 tsp. salt	5 g.
1 tsp. cinnamon	5 g.
¼ tsp. nutmeg	2 g.
1½ cups finely grated carrots (3 medium)	339 g.
¾ cup finely chopped pecans	169 g.

1. Preheat oven to 350°F (177°c)
2. Combine first 7 ingredients in a medium bowl
3. Sift next 5 dry ingredients together in a separate bowl
4. Add liquid mixture to dry ingredients all at once
5. Stir just until moistened, do not overmix
6. Fold in carrots and pecans
7. Spoon batter into greased muffin tins
8. Bake about 25 minutes or until firm

Carrot Zucchini Muffins

Ingredients: (makes 12)

1 cup sifted all purpose flour	226 g.
1/2 tbsp. baking powder	7 g.
1/2 tbsp. cinnamon	7 g.
1/2 tsp. salt	3 g.
1/4 tsp. baking soda	2 g.
1/8 tsp. nutmeg	1 g.
1 finely shredded zuchinni (3 ounces)	same
1 finely shredded carrot (3 ounces)	same
2 eggs	same
3/4 cup packed brown sugar	169 g.
1/3 cup vegetable oil	75 ml.
1/4 cup buttermilk	56 ml
1 tsp. vanilla	5 ml.
1/4 cup golden raisins	56 g.
1/4 cup chopped walnuts	56 g.

1. Preheat oven to 350°F (177°c)
2. Combine first 6 dry ingredients in a large bowl
3. Combine remaining ingredients together in a separate bowl, mix well
4. Add moist mixture to dry ingredients all at once
5. Stir just until dry ingredients are moistened
6. Spoon batter into well greased muffin cups
7. Bake for 30 minutes

Cheese Onion Muffins

Ingredients: (makes 12 large)

2 cups biscuit mix (bisquick) . . . . 452g.
2/3 cup milk. . . . . 151ml.
1 egg, beaten . . . . same
1/2 tsp. onion powder. . . . . 3g.
1/4 tsp. salt . . . . 2g.
1/2 cup grated cheddar cheese. . . . . 113g.
1/2 cup french fried onions (canned) crumbled. .113g.

1. Preheat oven to 400°F (204°C)
2. In a large bowl, combine all of the ingredients
3. Mix well
4. Spoon the batter into greased muffin tins
5. Bake for 12 to 15 minutes

Cherry Almond Muffins

Ingredients: (makes 12 large)

1/3 cup vegetable oil	75 ml.
1/2 tsp. almond flavor	3 ml.
2/3 cup sugar	151 g.
2 eggs	same
1 tsp. vanilla	5 ml.
2 cups all purpose flour,	452 g.
1 1/2 tbsp. baking powder	21 g.
1/4 tsp. salt	.2 g.
1/2 cup milk	113 ml.
1 cup halved, pitted, sweet black cherries	226 g.
1 1/2 tbsp. flour	21 g.
1/4 cup sliced almonds	56 g.

1. Preheat oven to 400°F (204°C)
2. In a large bowl, beat first 5 ingredients together
3. In another bowl sift next 3 ingredients together
4. Add the sifted dry ingredients to the first mixture alternately with the milk, stir until just combined
5. In a separate bowl dredge the cherries in the 1 1/2 tbsp. of flour
6. Fold the floured cherries, and the almonds into the batter. Spoon the batter into greased muffin cups
7. Bake about 20 minutes or until golden

Chocolate Bran Muffins

Ingredients: (makes 12 large)

1¾ cups all purpose flour	395g.
1 cup sugar.	226g.
½ cup cocoa	113g.
3 tbsp. baking powder.	14g.
1 tsp. salt.	5g.
1¼ cups raisin bran cereal.	282g.
1 cup milk.	226ml.
⅓ cup vegetable oil.	75ml.
2 eggs.	some
1 tsp. vanilla.	5ml

1. Preheat oven to 375°F (191°C)
2. In a large bowl sift first 5 ingredients together
3. Stir in raisin bran
4. Combine remaining ingredients in a separate bowl
5. Add liquid mixture to dry ingredients
6. Stir only until combined. (should be lumpy)
7. Fill well greased muffin cups ⅔ full
8. Bake 18 minutes until firm, remove while hot

Chocolate Chip Banana Muffins

Ingredients: (makes 12-14 large)

½ cup butter or margarine, softened . . . . 113 ml.

1 tsp. vanilla . . . . 5 ml.

¾ cup sugar . . . . 169 g.

2 eggs . . . . same

2 cups all purpose flour . . . . 452 g.

1 tsp. salt . . . . 5 g.

1 tsp. baking soda . . . . 5 g.

1 cup mashed ripe banana (about 3 medium) . . . 226 ml.

¾ cup semi sweet chocolate chips . . . . 169 g.

1. Preheat oven to 350°F (177°C)
2. In a large bowl, cream together first 3 ingredients, until fluffy
3. Beat in eggs one at a time
4. In a separate bowl, sift together next 3 dry - ingredients
5. Add sifted dry ingredients alternately with mashed banana to creamed mixture
6. Fold in chocolate chips
7. Spoon batter into well greased muffin cups
8. Bake 25 minutes or until firm

Chocolate Date Muffins

Ingredients: (makes 12)

1 cup boiling water	.226 ml.
3/4 cup chopped dates.	169 g.
1/4 cup shortening	.56 g.
1 cup sugar	.226 g.
1 egg	.same
1. tsp. vanilla.	.5 ml.
2 ounces melted chocolate, cooled	.56 ml.
2 cups sifted all purpose flour.	452 g.
1. tsp. baking soda	.5 g.
1/2 tsp. salt	3 g.
1/2 cup chopped walnuts	.113 g.

1. Preheat oven to 350°F (177°c)
2. In a small bowl, pour water over dates, set aside until lukewarm
3. In a separate large bowl, cream together next - 4 ingredients
4. Stir in cooled melted chocolate
5. In another bowl sift together flour, soda, and salt
6. Add sifted dry ingredients alternately with dates to the creamed mixture, beat well after each addition
7. Fold in walnuts
8. Spoon batter into well greased muffin tins
9. Bake 25 minutes until firm

Double Chocolate Muffins

Ingredients: (makes 12)

2 squares melted chocolate	56ml.
1/4 cup vegetable oil	56ml.
1 egg	same
1/2 cup buttermilk	113ml.
1/2 cup sour cream	113ml.
3/4 cup brown sugar	169g.
2 cups sifted all purpose flour	452g.
1 tbsp. baking powder	14g.
1/2 tsp. salt	3g.
1/2 cup semi sweet chocolate chips	113g.
1/4 cup maraschino cherries, drained and chopped	56g.

1. Preheat oven to 350°F (177°c)
2. In a small bowl mix chocolate and oil, set aside to cool
3. In a separate bowl combine next 4 ingredients
4. Add melted chocolate and oil
5. In a separate large bowl, combine flour, baking powder and salt
6. Add wet mixture to dry ingredients all at once
7. Stir just until moistened, do not overmix
8. Fold in chocolate chips and cherries
9. Spoon batter into well greased muffin tins
10. Bake 25 minutes or until firm

Chocolate Nut Muffins

Ingredients: (makes 12)

½ cup natural bran	113 g.
½ cup grape nuts cereal	113 g.
¾ cup milk	169 ml.
1 egg	same
⅓ cup vegetable oil	75 ml.
1 cup sifted pastry flour	226 g.
2½ tsp. baking powder	12 g.
½ tsp. salt	3 g.
¾ cup sugar	169 g.
¼ cup cocoa	56 g.
½ cup chopped pecans	113 g.
1 tsp. instant coffee	5 g.

1. Preheat oven to 400°F (204°C)
2. Combine first 3 ingredients in a large bowl, let stand until most of the milk is absorbed
3. Add egg and oil, beat well
4. In a separate bowl, sift next 5 ingredients together
5. Stir pecans and coffee into dry mixture
6. Add dry mix to moist ingredients
7. Stir just until combined
8. Spoon batter into greased muffin cups
9. Bake about 20 minutes or until firm

Cinnamon Flake Muffins

Ingredients: (makes 12)

2 cups cake flour	452 g.
3 tbsp. sugar	42 g.
1/2 tsp. salt	3 g.
1/2 tsp. cream of tartar	3 g.
4 tsp. baking powder	18 g.
1/2 cup shortening	113 ml.
2/3 cup milk	151 ml.
1/4 cup melted butter or margarine	56 ml.
1/4 cup sugar	56 ml.
1 tablespoon cinnamon	14 g.

1. Sift dry ingredients together
2. Cut in shortening until mixture is coarse crumbly
3. Add milk, stir well until dough follows fork
4. Turn dough out onto floured surface
5. Knead gently for 30 seconds
6. Roll dough 1/4 inch thick
7. Brush with melted butter and then sprinkle with 1/4 cup sugar and cinnamon
8. Cut dough into 2-inch strips
9. Stack strips 5 high
10. Cut off 2-inch pieces, and place cut side down in greased muffin pans
11. Bake at 425°F (218°c) for 12 minutes

Coffee Cake Muffins

Ingredients: (makes 12)

1 3/4 cups whole wheat flour, sifted . . . . 395 g.
1 tsp. baking powder . . . . .5 g.
1 tsp. baking soda . . . . .5 g.
1/8 tsp. salt . . . . .1 g.
1/2 cup softened butter or margarine . . . . .113 ml.
2/3 cup sugar . . . . .151 g.
2 eggs . . . . same
1 tsp. vanilla . . . . .5 ml.
1 cup sour cream . . . . .226 ml.
1/3 cup packed brown sugar . . . . .75 g.
1/2 cup bran flake cereal . . . . .113 g.
1/2 cup chopped nuts . . . . .113 g.
1 tsp. cinnamon . . . . .5 g.

1. Preheat oven to 350°F (177°C)
2. Combine first 4 ingredients, set aside
3. In a large bowl, beat next 4 ingredients together
   until fluffy
4. Alternately stir in the sour cream and the first mixture
   until blended
5. In a separate bowl, combine remaining ingredients for
   the filling. Butter the muffin tins well
6. Fill each tin 1/3 full with batter. Sprinkle 1 tsp. of filling into
   each cup. Fill each cup to 2/3 full with batter. Sprinkle
   remaining filling on top.
7. Bake for 20 to 25 minutes

Coffee Peanut Muffins

Ingredients: (makes 12 large)

2 cups all purpose flour	452 g.
1 tbsp. baking powder	14 g.
1 tsp. salt	5 g.
3/4 cup brown sugar	169 g.
3/4 cup peanut butter	169 ml.
2 eggs	same
3/4 cup milk	169 ml.
1 tsp. instant coffee	5 g.
1/2 cup cold water	113 ml.
1 tsp. cinnamon	5 g.
1/2 cup finely chopped peanuts	113 g.

1. Preheat oven to 400°F (204°C)
2. Combine first 4 ingredients in a bowl
3. Cut in peanutbutter until crumbly
4. Add next 5 ingredients
5. Stir just until ingredients are moistened
6. Fill greased muffin tins 2/3 full
7. Sprinkle with peanuts
8. Bake 20 to 25 minutes until tops are springy

Cottage Cheese Fruit Muffins

Ingredients: (makes 12 large)

1/4 cup butter, softened	.56ml.
1/2 cup firmly packed brown sugar	113g.
1/2 tsp. grated orange peel	.3g.
1/2 tsp. grated lemon rind	.3g.
1 egg.	.same
3/4 cup small curd cottage cheese.	.169ml.
3/4 cup sour cream.	.169ml.
1 1/4 cups unsifted flour.	.282g.
1 1/2 tsp. baking powder.	.8g.
1/2 tsp. baking soda	.3g.
1/2 tsp. salt.	.3g.
1/2 cup chopped dried apricots	113g.
1/2 cup chopped pitted dates	.113g.

1. Preheat oven to 350°F (177°c)
2. In a large bowl, beat first 4 ingredients until creamy
3. Mix in next 3 ingredients
4. In a separate bowl combine next 4 ingredients
5. Add apricots and dates to dry mixture, mix until
   well coated in flour
6. Add dry ingredients to beaten mixture
7. Stir until well blended
8. Spoon batter into greased muffin tins
9. Bake for 25 to 30 minutes

Cranberry Coconut Muffins

Ingredients: (makes 12 three inch)

2 cups all purpose flour	452 g.
1 tbsp. baking powder	14 g.
1 tsp. salt	5 g.
½ cup sugar	113 g.
1 tsp. cinnamon	5 g.
¼ tsp. nutmeg	2 g.
½ cup shredded sweet coconut	113 g.
2 eggs, beaten	same
1 cup buttermilk	226 ml.
¾ cup whole cranberry sauce	169 ml.
¼ cup vegetable oil	56 ml.

1. Sift first 6 ingredients together
2. Stir coconut into dry ingredients
3. In a separate bowl, combine eggs, milk, cranberry, and oil
4. Pour liquid mixture into dry ingredients
5. Stir lightly until just combined
6. Fill well greased muffin tins ¾ full
7. Bake at 400°F (204°c) 18 to 20 minutes

Cranberry Nectar Muffins

Ingredients: (makes 12)

1 3/4 cups flour, all purpose	395g.
1/2 cup sugar	113g.
2 1/2 tsp. baking powder	12g.
3/4 tsp. salt	4g.
1 egg	Same
3/4 cup apricot nectar	169ml.
3/4 cup whole cranberry sauce	169ml.
1/2 cup flaked coconut	113g.
1/3 cup vegetable oil	75ml.
1/2 tsp. coconut flavor	3ml.

1. Preheat oven to 400°F (204°C)
2. Combine first 4 ingredients in a large bowl
3. In a separate bowl combine remaining ingredients
4. Add liquid mixture to dry ingredients all at once
5. Stir only until moistened, do not overmix
6. Spoon batter into greased muffin cups
7. Bake for 20 to 25 minutes until firm

Cream Cheese Muffins

Ingredients: (makes 12 large)

1. 1/2 cup butter or margarine, melted . . . . 113 ml.
2. 8 oz. softened cream cheese . . . . 226 g.
3. 2 eggs . . . . same
4. 1/4 cup milk . . . . 56 ml.
5. 1 tsp. vanilla . . . . 5 ml.
6. 2 tbsp. raspberry or blackberry jam . . . . . .28 ml.
7. 1 3/4 cups sifted all purpose flour . . . . 395 g.
8. 1 tsp. baking powder . . . . 5 g.
9. 1/2 tsp. baking soda . . . . 3 g.
10. 1/4 tsp. salt . . . . 2 g.
11. 1/4 cup butter, softened . . . . 56 ml.
12. 6 tbsp. flour . . . . 84 g.
13. 1/4 cup brown sugar . . . . 56 g.
14. 1 tsp. cinnamon . . . . 5 g.

1. Preheat oven to 350°F (177°C)
2. In a large bowl, cream first 6 ingredients together
3. In another bowl, combine next 4 dry ingredients
4. Add the wet mixture to the dry, stir until combined only
5. Spoon batter into greased muffin cups
6. In another bowl, combine the remaining ingredients, mix until crumbly
7. Sprinkle topping evenly over 12 muffins
8. Bake for 20 to 25 minutes

Double Corn Muffins

Ingredients: (makes 12 medium)

1 1/4 cups all purpose flour sifted. . . . . .282 g.

1 tbsp. baking powder . . . . .14g.

1 tsp. salt . . . . 5g.

1/4 cup sugar . . . . 56g.

3/4 cup yellow cornmeal. . . . . 169g.

2 eggs, beaten . . . . same

1 cup milk . . . . 226 ml.

1/4 cup melted butter or margarine . . . . .56ml.

1/4 cup shelled, finely chopped, pumpkin or sunflower seeds

1 cup fresh cut corn kernels (about 2 ears). . . . 226g.

1. Preheat oven to 400°F (204°C)
2. In a large bowl combine first 5 ingredients, mix
3. In a separate bowl combine next 3 moist ingredients
4. Add to the dry mixture, stir just until moistened
5. Fold in remaining 2 ingredients
6. Spoon batter into greased muffin tins to 2/3 full
7. Bake about 25 minutes

Fruit Muffins

Ingredients: (makes 12 medium)

½ cup softened butter . . . . .113ml.

¾ cup sugar . . . . 169g.

1 tsp. vanilla . . . . .5ml.

⅔ cup yogurt . . . . 151ml.

1 egg, beaten . . . . same

1½ cups sifted all purpose flour . . . . 339g.

½ tsp. salt . . . . 3g.

2¼ tsp. baking powder . . . . 11g.

½ cup pitted, chopped, floured dates . . . . .113g.

1 cup chopped fruit, . . . (any combination of fruits)
                                                      226g.

1. Preheat oven to 350°F (177°c)
2. In a large bowl cream together first 3 ingredients
3. Add next 2 ingredients, mix well
4. In a separate bowl combine next 3 dry ingredients
5. Fold dry mixture into the first mixture
6. Stir just until combined
7. Fold in remaining ingredients
8. Spoon batter into greased muffin cups
9. Bake about 25 minutes or until done

German Apple Cake Muffins

Ingredients: (makes 12 large)

1 1 ¾ cups all purpose sifted flour. . . . . .395g.
2 ¾ cup sugar. . . . . .169g.
3 ¼ tsp. nutmeg . . . . .2g.
4 ½ tsp. cinnamon. . . . . .3g.
5 1 tsp. salt .5g.
6 4 tsp. baking powder . . . . .18g.
7 2 eggs. . . . . .same
8 ¼ cup melted shortening . . . . .56ml.
9 1 cup milk. .226ml.
10 1 tbsp lemon juice. . . . . .14ml.
11 1 tbsp grated orange peel. . . . . .14g.
   ¼ cup chopped nuts. . . . . .56g.
   1 cup chopped peeled apple . . . . .226g.
   3 tbsp. brown sugar. . . . . .42g.
   1 tbsp. flour . . . . .14g.

1. Preheat oven to 350°F (177°c)
2. Combine first 6 ingredients in a large bowl
3. In another bowl, combine next 5 ingredients
4. Add the moist mixture to the dry ingredients
5. Stir until just combined
6. Fold in the nuts
7. Spoon batter into greased muffin tins
8. Sprinkle with chopped apple
9. Combine last 2 ingredients in another small bowl
10. Sprinkle brown sugar-flour mixture over the apples
11. Bake about 30 minutes

66

Gingerbread Muffins

Ingredients: (makes 12)

½ cup sugar	113 ml.
½ cup shortening	113 ml.
½ cup molasses	113 ml.
2 eggs, beaten	same
1¾ cups sifted all purpose flour	395 g.
½ tsp. cinnamon	3 g.
½ tsp. ginger	3 g.
½ tsp. nutmeg	3 g.
¼ tsp. salt	2 g.
¼ cup buttermilk	56 ml.
½ tsp. baking soda	3 g.
½ tsp. hot water	3 ml.
½ tsp. vanilla	3 ml.
½ cup golden raisins	113 g.
½ cup chopped pecans	113 g.

1. Preheat oven to 375°F (190°C)
2. In a large bowl, cream first two ingredients together
3. Add next 2 ingredients, mix well
4. In a separate bowl, sift next 5 dry ingredients together
5. Add sifted dry mixture to first mixture alternately with buttermilk
6. Dissolve soda in hot water, add to batter and beat well
7. Stir in remaining ingredients
8. Spoon batter into greased muffin tins to ½ full
9. Bake about 30 minutes or until done

Honey Fruit Muffins

Ingredients: (makes 12)

1 cup all purpose flour.	226 g.
3/4 cups whole wheat flour.	169 g.
2 tsp. baking powder.	9 g.
1/2 tsp. salt.	3 g.
1 egg, beaten.	same
1/2 cup orange juice.	113 ml.
3/4 cup honey.	169 ml.
1/4 cup vegetable oil.	56 ml.
1/2 cup diced dry fruit.	113 ml.

1. Soak dry fruit in boiling water for 10 minutes, drain and reserve.
2. Preheat oven to 375°F (191°C)
3. Grease 12 muffin cups
4. Stir together first 4 ingredients in a large bowl
5. In a separate bowl, combine remaining ingredients
6. Add soaked fruit to liquid ingredients
7. Make a well in the centre of the dry ingredients
8. Add the liquid mixture all at once to the dry
9. Stir just until moistened, should be lumpy
10. Fill muffin cups and bake about 20 minutes until tops spring back when lightly touched

Hot Cheese Muffins

Ingredients: (makes 12)

2 cups sifted all purpose flour.	452g.
1/3 cup sugar.	75 g.
1 tbsp. baking powder.	14 g.
1/2 tsp. salt	3g.
1/8 tsp. cayenne	1g.
2/3 cup grated sharp Cheddar cheese	151g.
1 cup buttermilk	226 ml.
1/4 cup vegetable oil.	56ml.
1 egg, beaten.	same
1/2 cup golden raisins	113 g.
3 tbsp. grated sharp Cheddar.	42g.

1. Preheat oven to 425°F (218°C)
2. Sift first 5 ingredients together into a large bowl
3. Stir in cheddar
4. In a small bowl combine next 3 liquid ingredients
5. Add all at once to flour mixture
6. Stir just until combined; batter should be lumpy!
7. Fold in raisins
* 8. Spoon batter into greased muffin cups to 3/4 full
9. Bake about 20 minutes or until golden
10. Turn muffins out, sprinkle with grated Cheddar while still hot.

* When spooning batter into muffin cups; use the following method: use a 1/4 cup measure (not quite full) quickly dip batter into muffin cups filling each 3/4 full. Dip only once for each muffin cup!

71

Honey Glazed Bran Muffins

Ingredients: (makes 12)

1 cup natural bran	226g.
1 cup buttermilk	226ml.
1 cup sifted all purpose flour	226g.
1 tsp. cinnamon	.5g.
1 tsp. baking powder	.5g.
1/2 tsp. baking soda	.3g.
1/2 tsp. salt	.3g.
1/3 cup butter, softened	75ml.
1/2 cup brown sugar	113g.
1 egg	same
1/4 cup molasses	56ml.
1/3 cup currants	75g.
1/3 cup chopped dates	75g.
1/3 cup honey	75ml.
1 tbsp. corn syrup	14ml.
1 tsp. butter	.5ml.
1 tsp. lemon juice	.5ml.

1. Preheat oven to 400°F (204°c)
2. Combine first 2 ingredients in a large bowl
3. In a separate bowl combine next 5 dry ingredients
4. Add all at once to the bran mixture , stir just to mix
5. In a separate bowl cream next 4 ingredients together
6. Add to main mixture , fold in currants and dates
7. Fill greased muffin cups 3/4 full, bake 20 to 25 minutes
8. Combine remaining 4 ingredients in a small saucepan,
   bring to a boil on medium heat, reduce heat ,simmer 5 min.
9. Place cooled muffins one at a time in the glaze, set to dry

Lemon Muffins

Ingredients: (makes 12 large)

1 cup butter	226 ml.
1 cup sugar	226 g.
4 egg yolks	same
2 cups flour	452 g.
2 tsp. baking powder	9 g.
1 tsp. salt	5 g.
1/2 cup fresh lemon juice	113 ml.
4 stiffly beaten egg whites	same
2 tsp. grated lemon peel	9 g.

1. Preheat oven to 375°F (190°C)
2. Cream first 2 ingredients in a large bowl until smooth
3. Add egg yolks, beat until light
4. In a separate bowl sift next 3 dry ingredients together
5. Add the dry ingredients alternately with the lemon juice, to the creamed mixture, stir after each addition but do not overmix
6. Fold in stiffly beaten egg yolks and lemon peel
7. Spoon batter into greased muffin tins
8. Bake about 20 to 25 minutes

Lemon Cream Muffins

Ingredients: (makes 12)

1 1/4 cups flour. . . . . .282g.
1 1/2 tsp. baking powder. . . . . 8g.
1/2 tsp. salt . . . . 3g.
2/3 cup sugar. . . . . 151g.
1 4oz. pkg. cream cheese cut into 1/4 inch cubes. . . . . . 113g.
1 egg . . . . same
1/3 cup oil . . . . 75ml.
1/2 cup milk. . . . . .113ml.
1 tbsp. lemon juice. . . . . 14ml.
1 tbsp. grated lemon peel . . . . 14g.
1/4 cup chopped nuts . . . . 56g.
2 tbsp. lemon juice . . . . 28ml.
2 tbsp. sugar . . . . 28g.

1. Preheat oven to 375°F (190°C)
2. Sift first 3 ingredients together in a medium bowl
3. Add sugar, stir
4. Add cream cheese cubes, coat well in flour mixture
5. In a separate large bowl, combine next 5 ingredients
6. Add dry mixture to the moist ingredients
7. Stir until just combined
8. Fold in nuts
9. Spoon batter into 12 greased muffin tins
10. Bake 20 to 25 minutes
11. Combine remaining 2 ingredients, brush on hot muffins

Lemon Cornmeal Muffins

Ingredients: *(makes 18)*

2/3 cup vegetable oil	151ml.
1/2 cup sugar	113 g.
3 eggs	same
1 1/4 cups cornmeal	282g.
1 tbsp. grated lemon rind	14g.
1 1/2 cups sifted all purpose flour	339g.
1 tbsp. baking powder	14g.
1/2 tsp. baking soda	3g.
1/2 tsp. salt	3g.
1/4 cup lemon juice	56ml.
1 1/3 cups buttermilk	30/ml.
3/4 cup currants, dredged in flour	169g.

1. Preheat oven to 400°F (204°C)
2. In a large bowl combine oil and sugar, mix well
3. Beat in eggs one at a time, Stir in cornmeal, and rind
4. In a separate bowl sift together next 4 dry ingredients
5. Add 1/3 of the sifted dry ingredients to the moist batter
6. Add lemon juice and 1/2 of the buttermilk, mix slightly
7. Add another 1/3 of the sifted dry ingredients, mix slightly
8. Add the remaining buttermilk and sifted dry ingredients
9. Fold in floured currants
10. Spoon batter into well greased muffin tins
11. Bake for 20 to 25 minutes or until golden and firm

Luncheon Tomato Muffins

Ingredients: (makes 12 large)

2 cups flour. . . . . 452g.
1 tbsp. baking powder. . . . . 14g.
2 tbsp. sugar. . . . . 28g.
1/8 tsp. oregano. . . . . .1g.
1 tsp. salt. . . . . .5g.
1/2 cup shelled chopped pumpkin or sunflower seeds 113g.
1 egg. . . . . .same
1 (10oz.) tin, tomato soup . . . . 282ml.
1/4 cup melted shortening. . . . . 56ml.

1. Preheat oven to 425°F(218°C)
2. Sift first 5 dry ingredients together in a large bowl
3. Add seeds, mix
4. Combine remaining 3 ingredients in another bowl
5. Make a well in the dry ingredients, add the moist
   mixture all at once
6. Stir just until combined
7. Spoon batter into well greased muffin pans
8. Bake about 20 minutes

Maple Corn Muffins

Ingredients: (makes 16 small)

1 egg, beaten	same
1/2 cup buttermilk	113 ml.
3 tbsp. maple syrup	42 ml.
1/2 cup yellow cornmeal	113 g.
3/4 cup all purpose flour	169 g.
1 1/2 tsp. baking powder	8 g.
1/4 tsp. salt	2 g.
1/2 tsp cinnamon	3 g.
3 tbsp. melted butter or margarine	42 ml.

1. Preheat oven to 425°F (218°C)
2. In a medium bowl combine first 3 ingredients, mix well
3. In a separate large bowl combine next 5 ingredients
4. Add the first (liquid mixture) gradually to the dry mix
5. Add the melted butter, stir until just combined
6. Spoon batter into tiny well greased preheated tins
7. Bake 15 minutes or until crisp and golden brown

Maple Walnut Muffins

Ingredients: (makes 12 large)

½ cup maple syrup.	113 ml.
2 tbsp. melted butter.	28 ml.
¼ cup chopped walnuts.	56 g.
2 cups all purpose flour.	452 g.
1 tbsp. baking powder.	14 g.
1 tsp. salt.	5 g.
½ tsp. cinnamon	3 g.
1 cup milk.	226 ml.
3 tbsp. maple syrup :	42 ml.
¼ cup vegetable oil.	56 ml.
1 egg.	same
1 tbsp. grated lemon rind	14 g.

1. Grease muffin cups
2. Into each cup place, 2 tsp. maple syrup, ½ tsp. melted-butter, and 1 tsp. chopped nuts. Set aside.
3. Sift next 4 ingredients together
4. In another bowl, combine remaining ingredients
5. Add Liquid mix to dry ingredients all at once
6. Stir just to moisten
7. Fill tins ¾ full
8. Bake at 400°F (204°c) 20 to 25 minutes
9. Invert on a rack set on wax paper, let stand 3 minutes
10. Remove pan from inverted muffins

Mincemeat Muffins

Ingredients: (makes 12)

1 egg.	. . . . .same
1 tbsp. grated orange rind.	. . . . .14 g.
1/4 cup vegetable oil.	. . . . .56 ml.
1/2 cup conned mincemeat.	. . . . .113 ml.
3/4 cup apple juice.	. . . . .169 ml.
2 cups sifted cake flour.	. . . . .452 g.
1/4 cup sugar.	. . . . .56 g.
4 tsp. baking powder.	. . . . .18 g.
1/2 tsp. salt.	. . . . .3 g.

1. Beat egg lightly
2. Stir in next 4 ingredients
3. In a separate bowl, sift last 4 ingredients together
4. Blend dry ingredients into liquid mixture
5. Stir lightly until just combined
6. Fill greased muffin tins 3/4 full
7. Bake at 400°F (204°C) for 15 minutes or until springy

Mincemeat Oatmeal Muffins

Ingredients: (makes 12 medium)

1 3/4 cups all purpose flour	395g.
2 1/2 tsp. baking powder	12 g.
3/4 tsp. salt	5 g.
1/3 cup oatmeal	75g.
1 egg, beaten	same
3/4 cup milk	169ml.
1/3 cup vegetable oil	75ml.
1/2 cup mincemeat	113ml.
1/2 cup molasses	113ml.

1. Preheat oven to 400°F (204°c)
2. In a large bowl, sift first 3 ingredients together
3. Add oatmeal
4. In a separate bowl combine remaining ingredients
5. Add liquid mixture to dry ingredients all at once
6. Stir only until combined
7. Fill greased muffin cups with batter
8. Bake for 20 to 25 minutes until tops spring back

Mini Bran Muffins

Ingredients: (makes 20)

1½ cups natural bran . . . . 339g.
1 cup whole wheat flour. . . . . .226g.
½ cup raisins . . . . 113g.
¼ cup chopped pecans . . . . 56g.
1 tsp. baking soda. 5g.
1 tsp. cinnamon . . . . .5g.
1 tsp. nutmeg . . . . 5g.
1 egg, beaten. . . . . .same
⅔ cup honey. . . . . .151ml.
2 tbsp. vegetable oil. . . . . .28ml.
1 tsp. vanilla . . . . .5ml.
¾ cup skim milk. . . . . .169ml.

1. Preheat oven to 375°F (191°c)
2. Combine first 7 ingredients in a large bowl
3. In a separate bowl combine remaining ingredients
4. Add liquid mixture to dry ingredients all at once
5. Stir just until combined
6. Spoon batter into greased muffin tins, (about
   1 heaping tablespoon per muffin)
7. Bake for 12 to 15 minutes, until firm

Morning Glory Muffins

Ingredients: (makes 18)

2 cups all purpose flour	452 g.
1⅓ cups sugar	301 g.
2 tsp. baking soda	9 g.
2 tsp. cinnamon	9 g.
¼ tsp. nutmeg	2 g.
½ tsp. salt	3 g.
2 cups grated carrot	452 g.
½ cup raisins	113 g.
½ cup chopped pecans	113 g.
½ cup sweetened shredded coconut	113 g.
1 cup peeled, cored, and grated apple	226 g.
3 large eggs	same
¾ cup vegetable oil	169 ml.
¼ cup orange juice	56 ml.
2 tsp. vanilla	9 ml.

1. Preheat oven to 350°F (176°C)
2. Sift together first 6 ingredients in a large bowl
3. Stir in next 5 ingredients
4. In a separate bowl, beat eggs together with, oil, juice, and vanilla
5. Stir liquid mixture into flour mixture (lightly)
6. Spoon batter into well greased muffin tins (filled to the top)
7. Bake for 35 minutes or until springy to touch
8. Let cool for 5 minutes and then turn out on a rack

Mushroom Cheese Muffins

Ingredients: (makes 12 large)

2 cups sifted all purpose flour. . . . . .452g.
1/4 cup sugar. . . . . .56g.
1 tbsp. baking powder. . . . . 14g.
1 tsp. salt . . . . 5g.
1/4 tsp. onion powder. . . . . 2g.
1 can (4 oz.) sliced mushrooms (drained, reserve liquid)
1 tbsp. vegetable oil . . . . 14 ml.
1/4 cup mushroom liquid. . . . . .56ml.
3/4 cup milk . . . . 169ml.
1 egg, slightly beaten . . . . .same
1/2 cup grated brick cheese . . . . 113g.
1/4 cup melted butter or margarine . . . . 56ml.

1. Preheat oven to 400°F (204°c)
2. Combine first 5 ingredients in a large bowl, mix well
3. Drain the mushrooms, reserve 1/4 cup of the liquid
4. Sauté the mushrooms lightly in the oil
5. Combine remaining ingredients in a large bowl, mix well
6. Add the moist mixture to the first dry mixture
7. Stir just enough to moisten the dry ingredients
8. Fill greased muffin tins 2/3 full
9. Bake about 20 minutes

"Oatapple"-Raisin Muffins

Ingredients: (makes 12)

1 egg	. . . . Same
1 apple, chopped	. . . . .same
3/4 cup raisins	. . . . 169 g.
3/4 cup milk	. . . . 169 ml.
1/2 cup vegetable oil	. . . . 113 ml.
1 cup quick cooking oats	. . . . 226 g.
1 cup all purpose flour	. . . . 226 g.
1/3 cup sugar	. . . . 75 g.
1 tbsp. baking powder	. . . . 14 g.
1 tsp. salt	. . . . 5 g.
1 tsp. nutmeg	. . . . 5 g.
2 tsp. cinnamon	. . . . 9 g.

1. Beat egg, stir in remaining ingredients
   until well mixed
2. Fill 12 greased muffin cups 3/4 full with batter
3. Bake at 400°F (204°c) about 20 minutes

Oatmeal Prune Muffins

Ingredients: (makes 12)

1 cup flour, all purpose	226 g.
1/3 cup sugar.	75 g.
2 1/4 tsp. baking powder	11 g.
1 tsp. salt.	5 g.
1/2 tsp. baking soda.	3 g.
1 1/3 cups quick cooking oatmeal	301 g.
3/4 cup chopped pitted prunes.	169 g.
1 cup buttermilk.	226 ml.
1/4 cup melted butter, cooled.	56 ml.
1/4 cup molasses	56 ml.
1 egg, lightly beaten	same

1. Preheat oven to 400°F (204°c)
2. Sift together first 5 ingredients in a large bowl
3. Add oatmeal and prunes
4. In another bowl combine remaining ingredients
5. Add liquid mixture to dry, all at once
6. Stir just until combined
7. Spoon batter into greased muffin tins
8. Bake 25 minutes or until golden

Pear Muffins

Ingredients: (makes 12)

1 3/4 cups all purpose flour	395 g.
1/3 cup sugar	75 g.
2 1/2 tsp. baking powder	11 g.
3/4 tsp. salt	4 g.
1 egg	same
1/3 cup vegetable oil	75 ml.
3/4 cup chopped canned pears	169 g.
1/2 cup pear syrup	113 ml.
1/2 cup shredded cheddar cheese	113 g.
1/2 cup chopped filberts or walnuts	113 g.

1. Preheat oven to 400°F (204°C); grease muffin tins well
2. Combine first 4 ingredients in a large bowl
3. In a separate bowl, combine next 4 ingredients
4. Pour liquid mixture into dry all at once
5. Stir only until combined, do not overmix
6. Fold in cheese and nuts; spoon batter into greased tins
7. Bake 20 to 25 minutes until firm

Pineapple Bran Muffins

Ingredients: (makes 12)

1/3 cup crushed unsweetened pineapple, drained . . . . 75 ml.

enough pineapple syrup and orange juice to make 1 cup   226 ml.

1/2 cup bran cereal . . . . 113 g.

1 3/4 cups all purpose flour. . . . . 395 g.

1/2 cup sugar. . . . . 113 g.

2 1/2 tsp. baking powder. . . . . 12 g.

3/4 tsp. salt. . . . . 4 g.

1 egg . . . . same

1/3 cup vegetable oil . . . . 75 ml.

1/2 cup chopped pecans. . . . . 113 g.

1. Preheat oven to 400°F (204°C)
2. In a large bowl pour pineapple and 1 cup juice over the bran, let stand 10 minutes
3. In a separate bowl combine next 4 dry ingredients
4. Add egg, oil, and pecans to the pineapple bran mix
5. Add the entire moist mixture to the dry ingredients all at once
6. Stir just until combined, do not overmix
7. Spoon batter into greased muffin cups
8. Bake for 20 to 25 minutes, or until firm

Pineapple-Carrot-Date Muffins

Ingredients: (makes 12)

2 eggs. .same

2/3 cup firmly packed brown sugar . . . . .151 g.

1/3 cup vegetable oil . . . . .75 ml.

1/2 cup crushed unsweetened pineapple (in its own juice) 113 ml.

1/2 cup finely grated carrots (1 large). . . . . 113 g.

1/2 cup chopped dates. . . . . .113 g.

1/2 cup chopped walnuts . . . . .113 g.

1 1/2 cups sifted all purpose flour . . . . .239 g.

1 tsp. baking powder. . . . . .5 g.

1/2 tsp. baking soda. . . . . .3 g.

1 tsp. salt .5 g.

1. tsp. cinnamon . . . . .5 g.

1. cup rolled oats. . . . . .226 g.

1. Preheat oven to 375°F (190°C)
2. Combine first 7 ingredients in a large bowl
3. In a separate large bowl combine remaining
   dry ingredients
4. Add moist mixture to dry ingredients all at once
5. Stir just until dry ingredients are moistened
6. Spoon batter into greased muffin cups
7. Bake for 20 to 25 minutes

Pineapple Cheese Muffins

Ingredients: (makes 12)

2 cups sifted all purpose flour . . . . 452g.
3/4 cup sugar. . . . . 169g.
1 tbsp baking powder. . . . . 14g.
1/2 tsp. baking soda . . . . 3g.
1 tsp. salt .5g.
1 tsp. vanilla . . . . 5ml.
1 1/4 cups crushed pineapple. . . . . 282ml.
1/4 cup melted shortening . . . . 56ml.
2 eggs .same
1/2 cup finely grated cheddar cheese . . . . 113g.
1/2 cup chopped nuts. . . . . 113g.

1. Preheat oven to 350°F (177°c)
2. Sift first 5 ingredients together
3. In a separate bowl combine next 4 ingredients
4. Add moist mixture to dry ingredients all at once
5. Stir just until dry ingredients are moistened
6. Fold in cheese and nuts
7. Spoon butter into greased muffin tins
8. Bake for 25 to 30 minutes

Pineapple Corn Muffins

Ingredients: (makes 12)

1 cup yellow corn meal. . . . . .226g.
1 cup sifted all purpose flour. . . . . 226g.
1/3 cup sugar. . . . . 75g.
1 tbsp. baking powder. . . . . 14g.
1 tsp. salt. . . . . .5g.
1/4 cup vegetable oil. . . . . 56ml.
1 egg, beaten. . . . . same
1 cup crushed pineapple (reserve juice). . . . . 226ml.
1/2 cup pineapple juice. . . . . .113ml.

1. Preheat oven to 425°F (218°C)
2. In a large bowl, combine first 5 ingredients
3. In a separate bowl combine remaining ingredients
4. Add the moist mixture to the dry ingredients
5. Stir just until combined, do not overmix
6. Spoon batter into greased muffin tins
7. Bake for 15 to 20 minutes

Peach-Cheese Streusal Muffins

Ingredients: (makes 12)

1¾ cups sifted all purpose flour	395g.
½ cup sugar	113 g.
1 tbsp baking powder	14g.
⅛ tsp. nutmeg	1g.
¼ tsp. salt	2g.
½ cup finely shredded Monterey Jack (white) cheese . .	113g.
1 cup peeled diced peaches (1 medium)	226g.
1 tsp. grated lemon peel	5g.
1 egg, beaten	same
⅔ cup milk	151ml.
¼ cup vegetable oil	56ml.
¼ cup sugar	56g.
¼ cup chopped nuts	56g.
½ tbsp. butter or margarine, melted	7ml.
½ tsp. cinnamon	3ml.

1. Preheat oven to 400°F (204°C)
2. Combine first 5 ingredients in a large bowl
3. Stir in next 3 ingredients
4. Combine next 3 liquid ingredients in a separate bowl
5. Add liquid ingredients all at once to first mixture
6. Stir just until moistened, do not overmix
7. Spoon batter into well greased muffin tins
8. Combine remaining 4 ingredients for a topping
9. Sprinkle topping over muffins
10. Bake 20 to 25 minutes

Peach Pecan Muffins

Ingredients: (makes 12 three inch)

2 cups all purpose flour	. . . .	452g.
1 tbsp. baking powder	. . . .	14g.
1 tsp. salt	. . . .	5g.
1/2 cup sugar	. . . .	113g.
1 tsp. cinnamon	. . . .	5g.
1/4 tsp. nutmeg	. . . .	2g.
1/2 cup chopped pecans	. . . .	113g.
2 eggs, slightly beaten	. . . .	same
1 cup buttermilk	. . . .	226ml.
3/4 cup peeled, chopped peaches	. . . .	169g.
1/4 cup vegetable oil	. . . .	56ml.
1/4 cup sugar	. . . .	56g.
1 tsp cinnamon	. . . .	5g.
2 tbsp. chopped pecans (finely chopped)	. . . . . .	28g.

1. Preheat oven to 400°F (204°c)
2. Sift first 6 dry ingredients together in a large bowl
3. Stir in pecans
4. Combine next 4 moist ingredients together in a separate bowl
5. Pour liquid mixture into dry ingredients
6. Stir until just combined, but still lumpy
7. Fill greased muffin tins 3/4 full with batter
8. Combine remaining 3 ingredients for a topping
9. Sprinkle topping mixture over unbaked muffins
10. Bake for 20 minutes

Peach-Yogurt-Almond Muffins

Ingredients: (makes 12 large)

1 cup chopped peaches, drained and towel dried . . .	.226 g.
1 cup yogurt	.226 ml.
1 tbsp. lemon rind	14 g.
1 egg	same
3/4 cup honey	.169 ml.
1/4 cup melted butter	.56 ml.
2 cups all purpose flour, sifted	.452 g.
1 tbsp. baking powder	14 g.
1/2 tsp. baking soda	3 g.
1/4 tsp. salt	2 g.
1/2 cup sliced almonds	113 g.

1. Preheat oven to 375°F (190°C)
2. Combine first 6 ingredients in a bowl, mix well, set aside
3. Combine remaining ingredients in a large bowl, mix
4. Pour liquid mixture over flour mixture
5. Stir just until dry ingredients are moistened
6. Fill greased muffin cups 2/3 full
7. Bake for 25 minutes or until tops spring back
   when touched lightly.

Peanutbutter Apricot Muffins

Ingredients: (makes 12 large)

1¼ cups dried apricots	282 g.
2 eggs lightly beaten	same
1 cup yogurt	226ml.
½ cup molasses	113ml.
1 cup whole wheat flour	226 g.
½ cup all purpose flour	113 g.
2 tbsp. wheat germ	28 g.
½ tsp. salt	3 g.
1 tsp. baking soda	5 g.
½ tsp. nutmeg	3 g.
½ cup chunky peanut butter	113g.
1½ tbsp. sugar }topping	21g.
1 tsp. cinnamon	5 g.

1. Soak apricots in boiling water for 10 minutes
2. Drain apricots and chop fine, reserve
3. Preheat oven to 400°F (204°c)
4. Combine eggs, yogurt, and molasses in a bowl, reserve
5. In a large bowl combine next 6 dry ingredients
6. Cut peanutbutter into dry ingredients (until pea size)
7. Stir soaked apricots into peanutbutter mixture
8. Pour liquid mixture all at once into dry ingredients
9. Stir only until moistened, do not overmix
10. Spoon batter into greased muffin tins
11. Combine remaining ingredients for the topping and sprinkle on top of batter in each tin
12. Bake 18 to 20 minutes or until golden

Peanut butter Chip Muffins

Ingredients: (makes 12)

1¾ cups all purpose sifted flour	395g.
3½ tsp. baking powder	17g.
2 tbsp. sugar	28g.
¾ tsp. salt	4g.
2 tbsp. wheat germ	28g.
¼ cup soft shortening	56ml.
¼ cup peanut butter	56ml.
1 egg, beaten	same
¾ cup milk	151ml.
½ cup chocolate chips	113g.
½ cup peanut-butter chips	113g.
apricot preserves	same

1. Preheat oven to 400°F (204°C)
2. Sift first 4 ingredients together into a large bowl
3. Add wheat germ
4. Cut in shortening and peanut butter
5. In a separate bowl combine egg and milk
6. Add all at once to dry mixture, stir only until moistened
7. Fold in chips
8. Spoon batter into greased muffin cups
9. Place ½ tsp. of apricot preserve on top of each muffin, press in slightly
10. Bake about 25 minutes or until done

Peanut-Butter-Jam Muffins

Ingredients: (makes 12)

2 cups sifted all purpose flour . . . . 452g.
½ cup sugar. .113g.
2½ tsp. baking powder. . . . . 12g.
½ tsp. salt . . . . .3g.
½ cup chunky peanut butter . . . . .113g.
2 tbsp. butter or margarine. . . . . 28ml.
2 eggs, well beaten. . . . . .same
1 cup buttermilk . . . . .226ml.
¼ cup currant jelly, melted . . . . 56ml.
⅓ cup finely chopped toasted peanuts . . . . . . 75g.

1. Preheat oven to 400°F (204°c)
2. Sift first 4 ingredients together
3. Cut in next 2 ingredients until mixture resembles
   coarse crumbs
4. Add eggs and milk all at once
5. Stir just until dry ingredients are moistened
6. Spoon batter into greased muffin tins (⅔ full)
7. Bake 20 to 25 minutes
8. Immediately brush tops of muffins with melted jelly
9. Dip tops in chopped peanuts

Double Peanut Muffins

Ingredients: (makes 12 large)

2 cups sifted all purpose flour . . . . 452g.
1 tbsp. baking powder . . . . 14g.
1 tsp. salt . . . . 5g.
1 cup chunky peanut butter . . . . 226g.
2/3 cup sugar . . . . 151g.
2 eggs . . . . same
1 tbsp. grated orange rind . . . . 14g.
3/4 cup orange juice . . . . 169ml.
1/2 cup milk . . . . 113ml.
3/4 cup raisins . . . . 169g.
1/4 cup chopped peanuts . . . . 56g.
1/2 tsp. cinnamon . . . . 3g.
1 tbsp. sugar . . . . 14g.

1. Preheat oven to 350°F (177°c)
2. Combine first 3 ingredients in a large bowl
3. In a separate bowl combine next 7 ingredients
4. Add moist mixture to dry ingredients all at once
5. Stir just until dry ingredients are moistened
6. Spoon batter into greased muffin cups
7. Combine remaining ingredients for a topping
   and spread evenly over muffins before baking
8. Bake for 30 to 35 minutes

Prune-Apricot Streusal Muffins

Ingredients: (makes 12 large)

½ cup finely chopped, dried apricots . . . . .113g.

½ cup finely chopped, dried prunes . . . . .113g.

¾ cup sugar .169g.

¼ cup vegetable oil . . . . .56ml.

2 eggs . . . . .same

2 tsp. grated lemon peel . . . . .9ml.

2 cups sifted all purpose flour . . . . .452g.

1 tbsp. baking powder . . . . .14g.

½ tsp salt . . . . .3g.

¼ cup melted butter . . . . .56ml.

½ cup flour .113g.

¼ cup chopped pecans . . . . .56g.

2 tbsp. sugar . . . . .28g.

1. Preheat oven to 350°F (177°C)
2. Soak first 2 ingredients in hot water for 10 minutes then drain and reserve
3. In a large bowl combine next 4 ingredients
4. Add the pre-soaked fruits and mix well
5. In a separate large bowl combine the next 3 ingredients
6. Add the moist mixture to the dry ingredients
7. Stir just until combined, do not overmix
8. Spoon batter into greased muffin tins to ¾ full
9. In a separate bowl combine remaining ingredients, mix well
10. Sprinkle topping evenly amongst 12 muffins
11. Bake about 25 minutes

Prune Nut Muffins

Ingredients: (makes 12)

1 cup dried prunes, pitted and chopped . . . . . .226g.
2 tsp. shredded orange peel . . . . .9 g.
3/4 cup orange juice .169ml.
1/4 cup lemon juice . . . . 56ml.
2 cups sifted all purpose flour . . . . .452g.
3/4 cup sugar . . . . .169g.
1 tbsp. baking powder . . . . .14g.
1/2 tsp. salt . . . . .3g.
1/2 tsp. cinnamon . . . . .3g.
2 eggs, beaten . . . . same
2 tbsp. vegetable oil . . . . .28ml.
1/2 cup chopped walnuts . . . . .113 g.

1. Preheat oven to 350°F (177°c)
2. Combine first 4 ingredients, let stand 1/2 hour
3. Sift together next 5 dry ingredients in a large bowl
4. Add eggs and oil to prune mixture
5. Add entire moist mixture to dry ingredients
6. Stir just until dry ingredients are moistened
7. Fold in nuts
8. Spoon batter into well greased muffin tins
9. Bake for 25 minutes

Poppy Seed Muffins

Ingredients: (makes 12)

½ cup poppy seed	113 g.
¾ cup buttermilk	169 ml.
¾ cup sugar	169 g.
2 eggs	same
½ cup vegetable oil	113 ml.
½ tsp. vanilla	3 ml.
½ cup chopped walnuts	113 g.
1 tbsp. grated lemon rind	14 g.
2 cups sifted all purpose flour	452 g.
½ tsp. salt	3 g.
¾ tsp. baking soda	4 g.

1. Combine first 2 ingredients, let stand 2 hours
2. Preheat oven to 350°F (177°C)
3. In a separate bowl combine next 6 ingredients
4. Add poppy seed and buttermilk to moist mixture
5. In a separate large bowl combine 3 remaining ingredients
6. Add wet mixture to dry ingredients all at once
7. Stir just until dry ingredients are moistened
8. Spoon batter into greased muffin cups
9. Bake about 25 minutes or until firm

Pumpkin Cranberry Muffins

Ingredients: (makes 15 to 18)

3/4 cup brown sugar . . . . 169 g.
1/4 cup molasses . . . . 56 ml.
1/2 cup soft butter . . . . 113 ml.
1 egg, beaten . . . . same
2/3 cup mashed pumpkin . . . . 151 ml.
1/3 cup whole cranberry sauce . . . . 75 ml.
1 3/4 cups all purpose flour . . . . 395 g.
1 tsp. baking soda . . . . 5 g.
1/4 tsp. salt . . . . 2 g.
1/2 cup pecan halves . . . . 113 g.

1. Preheat oven to 375°F (190°C)
2. Cream first 3 ingredients together
3. Add next 3 ingredients, blend well
4. In a separate bowl, combine flour, soda, and salt
5. Beat dry ingredients into the moist mixture
6. Fold in pecans
7. Fill well greased muffin tins 3/4 full
8. Bake about 25 minutes or until firm

Pumpkin Seed Muffins

Ingredients: (makes 12 large)

1/2 cup shortening, melted	113 ml.
1 cup packed brown sugar	226 g.
2 eggs	same
1 cup canned pumpkin.	226 ml.
1/2 cup milk.	113 ml.
1 cup all purpose flour.	226 g.
1 cup whole wheat flour.	226 g.
2 1/2 tsp. baking powder.	12 g.
1/4 tsp. baking soda	2 g.
1/2 tsp. salt	3 g.
1 tsp. pumpkin pie spice.	5 g.
1/3 cup coarsely chopped pumpkin or sunflower seeds	75 g.

1. Preheat oven to 350°F (177°C)
2. Combine first 2 ingredients
3. Add eggs one at a time, beat well after each
4. Stir in pumpkin and milk
5. In a separate large bowl combine next 6 ingredients
6. Add moist mixture to dry ingredients all at once
7. Stir just until dry ingredients are moistened
8. Fold in seeds
9. Spoon batter into greased muffin cups
10. Bake for 30 minutes

Raspberry Nut Muffins

Ingredients: (makes 12 medium)

½ cup butter or margarine, melted	113 ml.
⅔ cup sugar	151 g.
1 tsp. vanilla	5 g.
1 tsp. grated lemon peel	5 g.
2 eggs	same
1½ cups, sifted all purpose flour	339 g.
½ tsp. salt	3 g.
½ tsp. cream of tartar	3 g.
¼ tsp. baking soda	2 g.
½ cup raspberry jam	113 ml.
⅓ cup dairy sour cream	75 ml.
½ cup chopped walnuts	113 g.

1. Preheat oven to 350°F (177°c)
2. Cream first 4 ingredients together until fluffy
3. Add eggs one at a time, beat well after each
4. In a separate large bowl, sift next 4 dry ingredients
5. In another small bowl, combine jam and sour cream, then add to the wet mixture
6. Add the entire moist mixture to the dry ingredients
7. Stir until just combined, do not overmix
8. Fold in the walnuts
9. Spoon batter into greased muffin tins
10. Bake for 25 to 30 minutes

Rhubarb Pecan Muffins

Ingredients: (makes 12 large)

1 cup whole wheat flour	226g.
1 cup all purpose flour	226g.
3/4 cup sugar	169g.
1 1/2 tsp. baking powder	8g.
1 tsp. salt	5g.
1/2 tsp. baking soda	3g.
1/4 cup vegetable oil	56ml.
2 tsp. grated orange rind	9g.
3/4 cup orange juice	169ml.
1 egg, beaten	same
1 1/4 cups finely chopped rhubarb	282g.
1/2 cup chopped pecans	113g.

1. Preheat oven to 350°F (177°c)
2. Combine first 6 ingredients in a large bowl
3. In a separate bowl, combine remaining ingredients
4. Add moist mixture to dry ingredients all at once
5. Stir just until dry ingredients are moistened
6. Spoon batter into greased muffin cups
7. Bake for 25 to 30 minutes

Rhubarb Streusal Muffins

Ingredients: (makes 12 large)

¼ cup sugar	56 g.
¼ cup chopped nuts	56 g.
½ tbsp. butter or margarine, melted	7 ml.
½ tsp. cinnamon	3 g.
1 cup firmly packed brown sugar	226 g.
¼ cup melted shortening	56 ml.
1 egg	same
¾ cup sour cream	169 ml.
2 cups sifted all purpose flour	452 g.
1 tsp. baking soda	5 g.
½ tsp. salt	3 g.
1¼ cups diced rhubarb	282 g.

1. Preheat oven to 350°F (177°c)
2. Combine first 4 ingredients (for topping), set aside
3. In a separate bowl combine next 4 ingredients
4. In another bowl combine flour, soda, and salt
5. Add moist mixture to dry ingredients all at once
6. Stir just until dry ingredients are moistened
7. Fold in rhubarb
8. Spoon batter into well greased muffin tins
9. Sprinkle topping over muffins
10. Bake 25 to 30 minutes, until firm

Rice Muffins

Ingredients: (makes 12 medium)

3/4 cup sifted all purpose flour. . . . . .169g.
1/2 tsp. salt. . . . . .3g.
1/8 tsp. baking soda . . . . .1g.
1/2 tsp. baking powder. . . . . .3g.
1/4 cup sugar. . . . . .56g.
2 eggs. . . . . .same
3/4 cup cooked rice . . . . .1.69g.
3 tbsp. melted margarine. . . . . .42ml.
1 cup sour cream . . . . .226ml.

1. Preheat oven to 350°F (177°c)
2. Combine first 5 ingredients in a large bowl, mix
3. In a separate bowl, combine remaining ingredients
4. Add the moist mixture to the dry ingredients
5. Stir just until combined, do not overmix
6. Spoon batter into greased muffin cups
7. Bake for 30 minutes

Rum Muffins

Ingredients: (makes 12 large)

1 egg lightly beaten.	Same
1 tsp. grated orange rind	5 g.
1/4 cup vegetable oil.	56 ml.
1/2 cup mincemeat	113 ml.
3/4 cup apple juice	169 ml.
1/2 tsp. rum extract.	3 ml.
2 cups sifted cake flour.	452 g.
1/4 cup sugar.	56 g.
4 tsp. baking powder	16 g.
1/2 tsp. salt	3 g.

1. Preheat oven to 400°F (204°C)
2. Grease 12 large muffin cups
3. Combine first 6 ingredients
4. Sift remaining ingredients together, into the liquid mixture
5. Stir just to blend, do not overmix
6. Fill muffin cups 2/3 full
7. Bake about 15 minutes or until tops spring back

Savory Potato Muffins

Ingredients: (makes 12 medium)

2 egg yolks, beaten . . . . same
2 1/2 cups peeled, finely grated red potatoes . . . . .565 ml.
3 tbsp. finely grated onion . . . . .42 g.
1/2 cup flour. . . . . .113 g.
1 tsp. salt .5 g.
1/2 tsp. pepper. . . . . .3 g.
1 1/2 tsp. baking powder. . . . . .8 g
1/4 cup melted butter, cooled . . . . .56 ml
2 egg whites. . . . . .same
pinch of salt . . . . .same

1. Preheat oven to 400°F (204°c)
2. Combine first 3 ingredients mix well
3. Sift next 4 dry ingredients into the moist mixture
4. Add melted butter, mix well
5. In another bowl, beat egg whites and salt until they hold stiff peaks
6. Fold stiffened whites into the potato mixture
7. Spoon batter into greased muffin cups to 2/3 full
8. Bake for 20 to 25 minutes or until puffed and browned

Southern Pecan Muffins

Ingredients: (makes 12 medium)

2 cups sifted all purpose flour . . . . 452 g.
2 tsp. baking powder . . . . 18 g.
½ tsp. baking soda . . . . 3 g.
½ tsp. salt . . . . 3 g.
½ tsp. cinnamon . . . . 3 g.
1 cup brown sugar . . . . 226 g.
1 egg, beaten . . . . same
1¼ cups buttermilk . . . . 282 ml.
3 tbsp. melted butter . . . . 42 ml.
1 cup coarsely chopped pecans . . . . 226 g.

1. Preheat oven to 350°F (177°c)
2. Sift first 5 ingredients together in a large bowl
3. Add sugar and mix
4. In a separate bowl combine next 3 ingredients
5. Pour the liquid mixture into the dry, all at once
6. Stir until just combined
7. Fold in pecans
8. Fill greased muffin tins to ¾ full
9. Bake for 25 to 30 minutes or until firm to touch

Spice Muffins

Ingredients: (makes 12)

2 cups sifted all purpose flour . . . . 452 g.
1/2 tsp. salt . . . . 3 g.
1 tsp. baking soda . . . . 5 g.
1/2 tsp. cinnamon . . . . 3 g.
1/2 tsp. nutmeg . . . . 3 g.
1/2 tsp. pumpkin pie spice . . . . 3 g.
1/4 cup sugar . . . . 56 g.
1 egg, beaten . . . . same
1/4 cup molasses . . . . 56 ml.
3 tbsp. vinegar . . . . 42 ml.
1/2 cup milk . . . . 113 ml.
1/3 cup vegetable oil . . . . 75 ml.
1/2 cup currants . . . . 113 g.

1. Preheat oven to 425°F (218°c)
2. Sift first 7 ingredients together, in a large bowl
3. Combine next 5 ingredients, in a separate bowl
4. Add liquid mixture all at once to dry ingredients
5. Stir only until combined
6. Fold in currants
7. Fill greased muffin cups 2/3 full with batter
8. Bake about 18 minutes or until firm

Streusal Marmalade Muffins

Ingredients: (makes 12 large)

¼ cup sugar		56g.
3 tbsp. all purpose flour		42g.
½ tsp. cinnamon	"TOPPING"	3g.
½ tsp nutmeg		3g.
2 tbsp. butter		28ml.
2 cups all purpose flour		452g.
¼ cup sugar		56g.
2 tsp. baking powder		9g.
¼ tsp. salt		2g.
¼ cup butter or margarine		56ml.
½ cup chopped pecans		113g.
1 egg, slightly beaten		same
½ cup orange juice		113ml.
½ cup orange marmalade		113ml.
1 tsp. lemon rind		5ml.

1. Preheat oven to 375°F (191°C)
2. In a small bowl combine first 4 ingredients; cut in butter
3. In a large bowl sift next 4 ingredients together
4. Cut in ¼ cup butter and stir in pecans
5. In another bowl, combine last 4 ingredients and add to the main dry mixture, stir just to moisten.
6. Spoon batter into well greased muffin tins.
7. Sprinkle with topping mix, bake 20 to 25 minutes
8. Remove from pans immediately

Sweet Potato Muffins

Ingredients: (makes 12)

1 3/4 cups sifted all purpose flour	395 g.
1 tsp. salt	5 g.
1 tbsp. baking powder	14 g.
1 tbsp. brown sugar	14 g.
1/2 cup coarsely chopped walnuts	113 g.
1/2 cup chopped floured dates	113 g.
2 eggs, beaten	same
3/4 cup milk	169 ml.
1 cup mashed cooked sweet potato	226 ml.
1/4 cup melted butter	56 ml.
Cinnamon	same
sugar	same

1. Preheat oven to 425°F (218°c)
2. Sift first 3 ingredients together in a large bowl
3. Add next 3 ingredients, mix well
4. In a separate bowl, combine next 4 ingredients
5. Add moist mixture to the dry ingredients
6. Stir just enough to moisten the dry ingredients
7. Fill greased muffin cups 2/3 full with batter
8. Bake about 25 minutes
9. While still warm, sprinkle tops with a mixture of cinnamon and sugar

Triple Treat Muffins

Ingredients: (makes 12)

2 cups flour . . . . 452 g.
1/4 cup sugar . . . . 56 g.
1 tbsp. baking powder . . . . 14 g.
3/4 tsp. salt . . . . 4 g.
1/4 cup sweetened cocoa . . . . 56 g.
1/4 cup chopped nuts . . . . 56 g.
1 egg . . . . same
1 1/4 cups buttermilk . . . . 282 ml.
1/4 cup butter or margarine . . . . 56 ml.
1/4 cup whole cranberry sauce, or jam of your choice
                                                        (56 ml.)

1. Preheat oven to 400°F (204°C)
2. Sift first 4 ingredients together in a large bowl
3. Divide sifted dry ingredients between 2 bowls
4. Stir cocoa and nuts into one of the bowls
5. In a separate bowl beat next 3 ingredients together
6. Add 1/2 of the liquid mixture to each of the 2 bowls
7. Stir each just until moistened, do not overmix
8. Grease muffin tins well, and place 1 heaping
   tablespoon of each batter side by side into tins
9. Make a small depression in each tin of batter
   and place 1/2 tsp. of cranberry or jam into it
10. Bake about 20 minutes

Whole Wheat Fruit Muffins

Ingredients: (makes 12 large)

1½ cups all purpose flour . . . . 339 g.
½ cup whole wheat flour . . . . 113 g.
¾ cup sugar . . . . 169 g.
1 tbsp. baking powder . . . . 14 g.
¼ tsp. salt . . . . 2 g.
½ cup oatmeal . . . . 113 g.
½ cup golden raisins . . . . 113 g.
¼ cup toasted sweetened coconut . . . . 56 g.
½ cup chopped dates . . . . 113 g.
¼ cup chopped pecans . . . . 56 g.
1 egg beaten . . . . same
1¼ cups milk . . . . 282 ml.
¼ cup vegetable oil . . . . 56 ml.

1. Preheat oven to 400°F (204°C)
2. Combine first 10 ingredients in a large bowl
3. In another bowl combine egg, milk, and oil
4. Add liquid mixture all at once to other ingredients
5. Stir just to moisten
6. Fill greased muffin tins ¾ full
7. Bake 20 to 25 minutes

Whole Wheat Orange Muffins

Ingredients: (makes 12)

2 cups whole wheat flour	452g.
2 tsp. baking powder	9g.
1/2 tsp. salt	3g.
1/2 cup packed brown sugar	113g.
juice of 1 orange, plus enough milk to make 1 cup . .	226ml.
skin of 1 orange, cut into small pieces (pith removed)	same
2 eggs	same
1/4 cup melted sweet butter	56ml.
1/2 tsp. orange extract	3ml.
2 tbsp. orange marmelade	28ml.

1. Preheat oven to 350°F (177°c)
2. Sift first 3 ingredients together into a large bowl
3. Add sugar and mix well
4. Place next 5 ingredients in a blender
5. Blend at low speed until orange rind is finely chopped
6. Add the liquid blend to the flour mixture
7. Stir just to moisten, batter should be lumpy
8. Spoon the batter into buttered muffin cups
9. Place 1/2 tsp. of orange marmelade into the center
   of each muffin (on top)
10. Bake about 25 minutes or until done

Yummy Trail Mix Muffins

Ingredients: (makes 12 large)

1 tbsp. instant coffee	14g.
1 1/4 cups boiling water	282ml.
3/4 cup chopped dates	169g.
2 eggs	same
1/2 cup chopped tart apple	113g.
1 cup deluxe trail mix (nuts and fruit) coarsely chopped	
3 tbsp. melted butter	42ml.
2 cups sifted all purpose flour	452g.
2 tsp. baking powder	9g.
1/2 tsp. baking soda	3g.
1/2 tsp. salt	3g.
3/4 cup brown sugar	169g.

1. Preheat oven to 350°F (177°c)
2. Dissolve coffee in water, pour over dates, set aside
3. In a medium bowl, combine next 4 ingredients, mix
4. Add the coffee-date mixture
5. In a separate large bowl, sift the next 4 dry - ingredients together
6. Add the brown sugar to the dry mixture; stir
7. Add the entire moist mixture to the dry ingredients
8. Stir just until combined, do not overmix
9. Spoon batter into greased muffin tins
10. Bake 25 to 30 minutes

Zucchini Muffins

Ingredients: (makes 12)

2 cups whole wheat flour	452g.
1 tbsp. baking powder	14g.
1 tsp. cinnamon	5g.
3/4 tsp. salt	4g.
2 eggs	same
3/4 cup milk	169ml.
1/3 cup oil	75ml.
1/2 cup honey	113ml.
1 tsp. lemon juice	5 ml.
1 tsp. lemon rind	5 g.
1 cup finely grated zucchini	226g.
2/3 cup seedless raisins	151g.

1. Preheat oven to 375°F (191°C)
2. Sift together first 4 ingredients in a large bowl
3. Combine next 6 ingredients in a separate bowl
4. Add moist mixture to dry ingredients all at once
5. Stir just enough to moisten dry ingredients
6. Fold in zucchini and raisins
7. Spoon batter into greased muffin cups
8. Bake 20 to 25 minutes or until golden

Basic Muffin Batter of The Nothing Muffin

1 cup all purpose flour
2 tsp baking powder
½ tsp salt
½ cup sugar
½ cup milk
¼ cup melted butter or margarine
1 egg

Stir together dry ingredients. Add melted butter and beaten egg to milk. Add liquid ingredients to dry, stirring only to moisten. To this batter, add anything, you have on the shelf — chocolate chips, butterscotch chips, peanut butter chips, fruit, nuts, etc.

Add nothing and serve with your scrambled eggs for breakfast with your favorite homemade jam or jelly.

Bake at 375 degrees F for 15 to 20 minutes. Yield — 8 medium muffins.

– RECIPES –

– RECIPES –